GLASS

from Antiquity
to the Renaissance

Giovanni Mariacher

GLASS
from Antiquity
to the Renaissance

CASSELL
LONDON

Cassell Publishers Limited
Artillery House, Artillery Row
London SW1P 1RT

Translated by Michael Cunningham from the Italian original
L'Arte del vetro: dall'Antichità al Rinascimento

© Gruppo Editoriale Fabbri, Bompiani, Sonzogno, Etas S.p.A., Milan 1966,
1984

This edition 1988

British Library Cataloguing in Publication Data
Mariacher, Giovanni
Glass from Antiquity to the Renaissance. — (Cassell's styles in art).
1. Glassware, to ca 1650
I. Title   II. L'Arte del vetro dall'Antichità al Rinascimento. *English*
748.29'01

ISBN 0-304-32186-9

Printed in Italy by Gruppo Editoriale Fabbri S.p.A., Milan

CONTENTS

Page

Artisans at work in a Bohemian glasswork, around 1420.
Miniature from a manuscript of *John Mandeville's Travels*.

9

INTRODUCTION

Glass is certainly one of the most exciting and impressive of all man's discoveries. Its origins, however, are shrouded in mystery, and experts still do not completely understand how it was first made. Nor is it known exactly where or when glass was discovered. A legend recorded by Pliny (*Historia Naturalis*, xxxvi 191) tells of a chance discovery by some Phoenician sailors: they were lighting a fire on a beach when they noticed a vitreous material forming among the embers. Like most legends, this probably contains an element of truth; for the basic component of glass is sand (silica), which is fused with an alkaline substance (soda) and lime (calcium carbonate). Furthermore, in the very earliest days of glass-making, the soda was taken from seaweed or coastal plants, which grew in abundance at the mouths of Phoenician rivers. The

Rhine

Aquileia
Adria
Ravenna
ITALY
Rome
Literno
Cumae Pompeii

Sicily

Early Glass Manufacturing Areas

13

Phoenicians were also great seafarers, which explains the early diffusion of glass around the Mediterranean.

At first, glass was most frequently used to make ornaments, since it was possible to colour glass pastes and apply them to small objects to make them look like precious stones. One of the earliest and easiest techniques for making real glass was baked glazing. The basic materials were melted and coloured; then the paste was dripped or poured into metal or terracotta moulds and made into small statues of animals and people, plaques, armlets and necklaces. To make hollow objects, the paste was placed around moulds which could afterwards be broken. This primitive glass paste was sometimes cut up into tiny pieces which were pierced and then strung together.

Glass-makers could not make larger and more beautiful objects until they were able to practise glass-blowing, which was probably discovered in Syria at the beginning of the Christian era. Blowing was carried out in this way: the amount of glass needed for the vessel was put at the end of a metal pipe about a yard long, and the craftsman blew the glass up to the size desired; then, with the help of a few instruments, he shaped and decorated the vessel. After this, he could apply colourants. The technique is virtually the same as that used today. The melting of the glass is done in wide, circular, stone pots with a number of openings for the blow-pipes in their sides. Glass is blown at extremely high temperatures; on the island of Murano, the famous glassworks in Venice, the pots are made of a fire-proof clay that can withstand a heat of up to 1400° centigrade. The first glass-blowers used moulds only occasionally, but nowadays moulds of metal or terracotta are always used to make large quantities of utilitarian glassware.

ANCIENT EGYPT

Until the invention of glass-blowing, glass-making developed slowly because glazing was the only process known. The Egyptians exported glass beads for many centuries; they were made very simply, by covering ordinary pebbles with a film of green or turquoise glass.

It is uncertain when real glass-making began. It

used to be thought that glass was first made during the 6th dynasty (2345–2181 BC), but it is more likely to have been at the beginning of the 18th dynasty (1567–1320 BC). The most characteristic examples from this period are perfume containers that look like small vases of various types: the bowl has a wide base and two handles, the *oenochoe* has a curved handle and a spout, the popular *alabastron* is cylindrical, and the amphora has two handles, a tapering bottom and no legs. Talismans, scarabs and small decorative masks were also brilliantly coloured with glazes. Many objects were produced for women, and glass was used to make anything from bracelets and clasps to necklaces of multicoloured beads. It could also be used to make clothes: this was done by stringing together tiny beads to make a kind of fabric, pieces of which have been found in tombs.

Glazing was done either by putting glass pastes on objects that were already moulded, for example, small statues of idols, animals and mythical characters, or by pouring the glass into moulds; small vases, goblets and other hollow vessels were made by this process. The distinctive features of this type of glassware were the way it was made and the colours, which were brilliant though few in number. The body of the vessel was usually dark or light blue, and about it were wound zig-zagging glass threads in orange or bright red, similar to those found on ointment jars. 'Trailing', as this process was called, was done with a kind of metal comb that traced the threads as the vessel was rotated. This kind of ware must have been made as early as the 4th or 3rd centuries BC, and not only in Egypt but also in nearby lands on the Mediterranean coast. Sea trade with Phoenicia further popularised glass-making, and after the Persians conquered Egypt glass began to be made in Babylon. It even began to be made in Etruria. Egyptian glass continued to be made in the Hellenistic and Roman periods, though by then the most refined glass was being made in Alexandria, the greatest port in the Mediterranean.

THE MIDDLE EAST

In the centuries before the birth of Christ, large quantities of glassware were made in Greece, on the

islands of Ionia and Cyprus, in Phoenicia and in
Mesopotamia. Syria was even more productive; some
Phoenicians in fact lived on the Syrian coast, and at
the mouth of the river Belus was the priceless flinty
sand used in making glass. Pliny considered the Syrian
towns of Tyre and Sidon the principal glass-producing
centres, calling the latter '*Sido artifex vitri*' ('Sidon the
town of the glass craftsmen').

The decisive event in the history of glass was the
development of glass-blowing in about the 1st century
AD. New technical and artistic possibilities appeared;
glass now began to become more refined in texture,
no longer opaque but colourless and transparent. As
for raw materials, silica was easily available and potash
could be taken from sea-plants; the wood of coastal
plants was used as fuel in the furnaces. As a result of
technical advances, bright colours and impastation
(the use of thick layers of colour) could be employed in
decoration. For centuries, Middle Eastern glassware
of all kinds was of astonishing beauty; Syrian work
was particularly outstanding. Glass-blowers soon
learned to make a large number of forms freehand,
some of them apparently influenced by cylindrical

ointment jars from Egypt (in that some were made in pairs and some had handles or special borders so that they could be hung on the wall). These and other designs – bird-shaped phials, small spherical vases, small amphoras and so on – have been discovered over a wide area, demonstrating how quickly the art of glass-blowing spread around the Mediterranean.

Before long, however, a new method of moulding was perfected. The glass was blown into moulds (probably made of terracotta); finishing touches could be added later, although this was rarely done. The craftsman worked freehand only when attaching handles or adding decorations. These were executed in several colours – blue, dark green, milky white or violet. The range of designs is quite remarkable, considering that the objects made were merely every-day containers for oils, ointments and perfumes. There was also a wide variety of shapes: some pieces were many-sided; some looked like fruit (bunches of grapes, or dates); some small bottles had a human face at the bottom, and some had one on either side, depicting Medusa, Bacchus, Ariadne and other mytho-logical figures. The most characteristic Syrian glassware was probably made by this particular technique.

Syria seems to have been the first country to produce long bottles with square bases and rather narrow necks, the bases decorated underneath with relief designs, which often depicted the god Mercury; they sometimes bore initials and seals, the equivalents of trade marks. Complete names, such as Ennion and Artas have also been found on early Syrian glassware; the fact that the only glass-makers of the time that we know anything about had Greek names suggests that they lived in a Greek colony in Asia Minor. The glass from which these objects were made was usually unrefined, and its rather dull green indicates that very large quantities were made for purely utilitarian purposes. Such pieces are now covered with lines because of chemical changes that took place while they were buried. Most of them have been discovered in tombs, since a dead man was usually buried with phials, ointment bottles, and other things that had been close or dear to him.

Another type of moulded vessel was the gladiator's glass, also known as the sportsman's glass or the circus glass. It was usually conical (although some examples are cylindrical), and was decorated in relief with small branches of palm-trees, crowns and inscriptions. The use of Greek in these inscriptions means that it certainly came from the Aegean area, the Greek colonies in Asia Minor, or Cyprus (an island long famous for its glass). Some also came from the west – from the Dalmatian coast and from northern Italy. There is good reason to believe that glass was well established commercially by about the 1st century BC, if only because of the themes – gladiator fights, chariot races, the circus – of the moulded decorations.

GLASS IN ROMAN TIMES

With the extension of the Roman Empire throughout the Mediterranean, the glass industry entered a new phase. One of the most productive areas was the province south of Rome called Campania, and in particular the towns of Pompeii, Pozzuoli, Literno and Cuma. In the north of Italy, there was a glassworks at Aquileia (a flourishing port and the nearest town to what was later to be Venice) and possibly at Adria. The establishment of a glass industry was encouraged even in the colonies of the Empire, especially in Gaul, the Iberian Peninsula and the German territories along the Rhine (where potash was abundant).

Although the Middle East, Phoenicia, Greece and Macedonia continued to produce large quantities of glass, Roman glass was clearly in the ascendant in the 2nd and 3rd centuries AD. The finest works were made for the rich of towns like Rome and Pompeii; indeed, high-quality work became a speciality of certain places, particularly Alexandria, while small centres in Italy and other parts of the Empire concentrated on the production of utilitarian items. But the similarity between Roman glass and the glass produced in the most distant outposts of the Empire is very striking. One reason is that the Romans tended to impose their way of life on all the peoples they conquered; the tableware of Rome, for example, became the tableware of the Empire. (Sometimes, of course, the influence was in the opposite direction: the Romans, as is well known, took over and disseminated the forms of Greek art and literature.) The uniformity achieved is more striking in the case of glass because it had not previously been used to make pitchers, vases and plates. These objects which had been made of clay or metal were now made of glass, decorated in very similar ways, and used for exactly the same purposes. Their shapes and designs were transmitted from region to region as the Empire expanded.

Pliny's account of the discovery of glass has already been given. He says that Syria was particularly rich in the basic materials, and also discusses Roman techniques, the composition of glass and the use of manganese dioxide, which he calls *'magnus lapis'*. It is now called glass-maker's manganese, and is used to rid the glass of impurities, thus ensuring that it is transparent. To judge from Pliny's writings, the great glass-blowers of Antiquity were acquainted with all the techniques used today, including the use of molten glass and the art of moulding with a grindstone or a lathe. Nevertheless, references to Roman glass-making are so sparse and obscure that it is impossible to be certain about any aspect of it, least of all the techniques employed.

The Romans divided glass into two groups: glass

for display and mass-produced, functional ware. The first category was expensive: Pliny tells the story of two *pterotos* cups (small cups with wings or handles) that were sold in the reign of Nero for no less than 6,000 sesterces. He also writes about what he calls 'Murrhine vases'. Although they were greatly admired in Rome and only the most distinguished glass-makers were asked to make them, we do not know exactly how they were made. The expression is generally accepted as describing an elegant, brightly coloured goblet or cup which was bowl-shaped and had no legs. The semi-transparent background was made up of coloured strips of glass that were placed together and then heated so that they fused. The final polishing of the vessel was done with a grindstone. The technique was also used to make pear-shaped phials for ointments, small cylindrical vases with lids like small pyxes (vessels containing the Host), plates and cupping-glasses which were either smooth or covered on the outside with ribs arranged like the rays of a monstrance. The background was usually amethyst red, bright blue, emerald green, yellow ochre or pale yellow, and contrasted strongly with the many gay colours of the decoration (milky white, light pink, etc). A very fine border in the form of a twisted thread was sometimes soldered on, and was later to inspire Murano filigree (lace-work design). A by-product of the glass pastes used in these decorations were *tesserae*, the small cubes used to make Roman and Byzantine mosaics.

A paste that looked like the one used in ordinary mosaics, but produced quite differently, was a molten mosaic paste. It was made almost exclusively in Alexandria, and was used to make decorations of animals, plants and geometrical designs, to imitate all kinds of precious stones, to produce striped impastation, and to make wall decorations and small sculptures which could later be smoothed down with a grindstone. The golden age of this type of glass was probably in the 2nd and 1st centuries BC, and the greatest glass-makers were Alexandrians, although many of them took the secrets of their trade to Rome and started a school there. It is said that when Augustus conquered Alexandria, some of the tribute was paid in glass.

One of the most famous Alexandrian products was cameo glass, sometimes called *vasa toreumata* (a vase decorated in relief). It was made by putting a dark opaque vessel, partly cooled, into white glass paste; when the outside had been engraved, it stood out against the dark background, producing a cameo-like effect clearly inspired by the designs of precious stones. The most celebrated examples of this technique are the Portland Vase, found near Rome in the 16th century and named after the man who presented it to the British Museum, and a vase depicting cupids gathering grapes, found at Pompeii and now in the Museo Nazionale, Naples.

Another important Alexandrian development was *diatreta* (reticulated) glass. The glass was usually transparent, had only one colour and was sometimes as clear as crystal. It was made by driving an engraving wheel deep into the glass, dividing it into two layers which were only held together by a few 'bridges'. The designs were highly imaginative, sometimes with a picture of a procession or a hunting scene; in this respect *diatreta* resembled Venetian *situlas*.

Syria, the birthplace of glass-blowing, was probably the first country to produce utilitarian glassware. A wide range of tools and the simplicity of the manufacturing processes made it possible to manufacture glass in abundance for secular or sacred purposes. Moulds of terracotta, stone and metal were frequently though not exclusively used, and glass made in this way was functional as well as attractive. Metal moulds had a great commercial potential, and the Romans were quick to make use of them.

From about the 1st–2nd centuries AD the glass industry entered a new phase. For economic reasons, the quality of the glass was poor – it was often green or even brown because of impurities and metallic oxide – but it was both elegant and useful. The most popular items were bottles for water or wine, oil cruets, tiny ointment phials, plates, saucers, glasses, cups with and without feet, cylindrical vases and vases with square bases with or without lids. There were also bottles for bath oils copied from the Greek vessel called an *ariballos*. Certain details were purely functional: handles, pedestals, the feet of cups, bottlenecks, lids, spouts. There were also smaller objects like drinking-straws, dropping-bottles and small portable flasks. By the 2nd and 3rd centuries AD glass was lighter and cheaper than terracotta and metal; but although basins, thick flat trays, pans with handles and cups began to be made in glass, their designs continued to be influenced by those traditionally used on the older materials.

Table glasses of the period are particularly interesting. Some had very thin undulating sides, some had consistently thick sides, some were conical, some had no legs and were almost bowl-shaped. Another common type was of a very pronounced cone-shape with a moulded symmetrical design. On the whole, there was little decoration since this glass was for domestic use. One interesting Alexandrian custom, though, was to use a grindstone to make a cup or vase smooth and trace a few parallel lines; light green or blue glassware that was squat and conical in design was usually decorated in this way. In the 3rd century or even earlier, glass threads were often trailed in a spiral design around the brims and bases of vessels; the threads were usually blue or milky white, the same colour as the background. This technique was sometimes used to add bosses, studs showing heads of lions and people, and skilfully fashioned grotesques. Alexandrian drinking-glasses and cups were not very elaborately designed, but they were refined and tasteful. They anticipate the techniques and florid styles of the Early Christian era, and Renaissance *graffito* work. In much the same way, the brightly coloured pictures of plants and animals on certain other 1st- and 2nd-century glass objects anticipate the huge frescoes at Pompeii and Herculaneum.

Throughout the Roman period, Egypt and Syria continued to produce large quantities of glass, but before the fall of the Empire it had begun to be made in many parts of Europe, though some of it was rather derivative. There is evidence that there were glass-works in Dalmatia, Illyria, Spain, Britain, Germany, Scandinavia and even the south of Russia. Their products gradually became increasingly dissimilar, and local styles began to appear.

LATE ROMAN AND EARLY CHRISTIAN GLASS

Glass-making continued after the disintegration of the Roman Empire, but it began to display greater regional variations. In particular, the cultural estrangement between east and west became more marked: eastern designs were preserved in the lands ruled by Byzantium, Roman designs were jealously guarded in western countries.

The Classical tradition persisted in the west. The design and engraved decoration of religious glassware in the Christian era were strongly influenced by traditional styles; on *diatreta* glass, for example, pagan mythology gave way to Christian iconography, but the technique remained unaltered. Imitation *diatreta* came into vogue in the Early Christian period. It looked very much like the original, but was made slightly differently; and the relief decoration was moulded separately and then attached. The best examples are the goblets and chalices found in Roman tombs. This technique was the predecessor of other methods of relief decoration, and began to be very popular in the northern areas of what had been the Empire.

All the same, the old art of engraving, particularly the simple technique of *graffito*, thrived: goblets, cups with and without feet, plates and so on were decorated in this way with names, inscriptions and religious or secular motifs. The religious motifs were of course used only on chalices and baptismal cups. The Vatican Museum in Rome has some superb 4th-century glass with engravings of Christ and the Apostles and scenes from the Old and New Testaments, including the baptism and confirmation of Christ. In general, however, the glass of the Early Christian era was unimaginative. One type was a phial said to contain the blood of a martyr, but it was nonetheless a small utilitarian vase, made of impure glass and poorly decorated. Otherwise, Early Christian glass mainly consisted of hanging lamps, pitchers, flasks, bottles and devotional vases.

In the 3rd and 4th centuries, a technique that had been popular in pagan times was revived: it was sometimes called tomb glass because it was found in the catacombs, or spherical glass because of its shape, but the usual name is gold glass. Green, red or dark blue glass was covered with gold leaf which was then decorated by *graffito;* then another piece of glass was soldered on top. The engravings on the gold were usually religious scenes or portraits of saints, but there were occasionally hunting scenes, portrait busts and pictures of a young man and woman (on a vessel probably intended as a marriage cup). The glass usually also carried writing, thick lines, stylised emblems and Christian symbols like the cross or the fish. A great deal of gold glass has been found in Roman and Jewish catacombs.

1. Amphoras and ointment jars. Greek, Egyptian, Roman, Palestinian. 5th century BC-4th century AD. Museo di Capodimonte, Naples.

2. Decorative sheet of glass. Roman-Alexandrian. 1st century AD. Victoria and Albert Museum, London. Photo: John Webb.

3. Necklace. Roman-Alexandrian. 1st century AD. Museo
Vetrario, Murano.

4. Pair of vases. Pre-Roman. 4th-3rd century BC. Museo Civico, Adria.

5. Vase. Alexandrian or Syrian. *c.* 1st century AD.
Museo Vetrario, Murano.

6. Plaque. Roman-Alexandrian (?). 1st-2nd century AD.
Victoria and Albert Museum, London. Photo: John Webb.

7. Bowl with two handles. Made by Aristeas. Syrian. Late 1st century AD. Castello Strada, Scaldasole, Pavia.

8. Bowl with two handles. Alexandrian. 1st century AD. Museo Civico, Adria.

9. Bowl. Alexandrian. 1st century AD. Museo Vetrario, Murano.

10. Pitcher. Roman. 1st century AD. Museo Civico, Adria.

11. Vase. Roman. 2nd-3rd century AD. Victoria and Albert Museum, London. Photo: John Webb.

12. Oil jar. Roman-Syrian. 1st-2nd century AD. Museo
Vetrario, Murano.

13. Glass. Roman. 1st-2nd century AD. Museo Vetrario, Murano.

14. Glass. Syrian. 1st century AD. Museo Vetrario, Murano.

15. Drinking horn. Roman. 1st century AD. Museo Civico, Adria.

16. Amphora. Phoenician. 6th century BC. Museo Civico, Bologna. Photo: Fotofast.

BYZANTIUM AND THE MIDDLE EAST

Western European glass began to display some originality towards the end of the Roman Empire, and was even to exert some influence on Medieval styles. The Byzantine Empire, however, remained faithful to Hellenistic and Alexandrian traditions, developing them with great refinement.

In addition to being the capital of the Eastern Roman Empire, Constantinople was the intermediary between East and West. The effects were seen in southern Italy, Sicily, Ravenna and later Venice, all of which had strong links with Constantinople, either because for a period part of the Byzantine Empire or because of their commercial contacts with it.

There is very little Byzantine glassware extant; most of what survives was brought back by the Venetians after the conquest of Byzantium and is now in the treasury of St Mark's. Perhaps the most beautiful example is a 5th-century violet *situla* (a vase shaped rather like a bucket) made of extremely thick glass with fine engravings of Bacchanalian scenes done with a grindstone. There is also a 6th-century circular hanging lamp made of glass as clear as crystal and decorated with circles and dots in relief. Another priceless piece is a dark violet goblet with glazed decorations of mythological characters surrounded by circles and other brightly coloured geometrical designs. Finally there are conical glasses of the Alexandrian-Hellenistic type, decorated with scenes from the *Iliad*.

ISLAMIC GLASS

Under the Abbasid caliphate (AD 750–1258), Islamic glass-production became of some importance. Emphasis was placed upon elegance, and glass came to be considered as priceless as rock crystal or precious stones. In about the 9th century, the most important glass centre was Samarra, a city on the Tigris in what we now call Iraq; it had great influence on techniques and styles in other Moslem areas, notably Persia, Egypt and Syria. The simple engraving on 9th-century Islamic goblets and bottles was itself inspired by the figurative designs of Sassanian glass. The glass that these vessels were made of resembled rock crystal in its thickness and precious stones in its dark colours. The imitation of precious stones was common in Islamic art, and some of these imitations were accepted in the West as works of exceptional beauty; one of these is the 10th-century sacred bowl in the Treasury of Genoa Cathedral.

Islamic craftsmen were very skilled at painting by means of glazing. From the 9th to the 12th century they simply copied the decorations on contemporary Egyptian and Persian ceramics, though the effects were very beautiful. Some of the best work of this type was done in the town of Rakka; Rakka glass, as it was called, was colourless or tinged with green, and had small designs or inscriptions in white, blue or gold enamel. It was also exported in the 13th century with Christian decorations and Latin inscriptions. Another important kind of glass with a glazed design was made in the Mosul and Baghdad region; it was called Aleppo glass. This was violet or blue, and had geometrical and floral designs, inscriptions and heraldic signs.

Damascus glass was popular throughout the Middle East from the end of the 13th to the beginning of the 15th century. The best-known examples are the mosque lamps, which are easily recognisable from the shape (like a vase or long bulb), the narrow neck, the small glass rings in the middle, and the conical base. They were decorated with wavy lines or extracts from the Koran, usually in blue, dark red, green and gold; the decoration was never representational because of the Koranic prohibition. Mosque lamps probably came originally from Syria, although some have been found in Egyptian mosques. They are easy to date because of the inscriptions and heraldic signs.

Bulb-shaped bottles, pilgrims' flasks, vases and goblets were also made in Damascus glass, and there were cups with long conical legs that may well have been the forerunners of Venetian Renaissance goblets. The glazed decorations were executed with the skill of a miniaturist, in bright colours and usually on a transparent background; they depicted such scenes as battles and processions of warriors. (Inevitably the prohibition of representation was less stringently enforced in the case of objects for secular use.) A certain amount of Chinese influence is discernible in the figurative decoration of this glassware; this is attributable to the establishment of Mongol dynasties within Islam.

Glass for everyday use was blue-green, but the decorations (festoons and coloured borders in relief) indicate that the influence of the late Roman period was still strong. A great deal of Damascus glass is on show in Tel-Aviv and at the Metropolitan Museum in New York. At the end of the 15th century, Islamic influence began to decline, in glass as well as in other fields; this coincided with the growing importance of Venetian glass.

CHINESE GLASS

A great deal of early glass which has been found in China is Western in origin and was evidently imported from Europe even as early as the 4th century BC. In tombs of this period glass beads and ornamental plaques which are definitely Western in origin have been discovered alongside others which have proved to be of Chinese manufacture.

During the Han dynasty (206 BC–220 AD) small glass animals modelled in a typically Chinese style appear to have been used as a cheap substitute for jade. Since there was a constant flow of Roman and Islamic glass into China brought by European traders, it was inevitable that many of the secrets of glass manufacture would eventually make their way East. Tradition has it that glass-blowing was introduced by Europeans in the 5th century but Chinese production seems to have been limited either to imitations of Western designs or to copies of articles which were more usually made in ceramics or stone.

In spite of the long tradition of glass manufacture, the Chinese do not appear to have appreciated glass for its own sake, and as a result there is little evidence of any really creative production.

GLASS IN WESTERN EUROPE DURING THE MIDDLE AGES

Early Medieval glass was for everyday use rather than display. One reason for this was the development of wine-making along the Rhine, the Meuse, the Rhône and the Seine, where glass was used for making bottles and drinking-cups. This impure glass was slightly green or blue, and the designs were copied from metal or terracotta models. It was decorated either by glazing straight or twisted threads made of the same kind of glass or by adding simple relief designs like bosses. Such work was of poor artistic quality; there was little of the elegance characteristic of Middle Eastern glassware, and the use of the grindstone was almost unknown. The main centres and developments were in the areas ruled by the Franks: in the Merovingian period (*c.* 500–*c.* 750), late Roman influence appeared in the design of small spherical bottles and flasks, and long conical or slightly tapering glasses; they also closely resembled contemporary miniatures.

From the middle of the 9th century to the Renaissance, the most productive, original and technically advanced areas were France (the Pyrenees, Normandy, Provence and Lorraine), the Low Countries (Liège and Brussels) and the south of Germany (Silesia, Thuringia, Saxony and Bavaria). A Teutonic style began to emerge; it was very different from the Classical style, and was until recently considered unimportant and mediocre. The glass was greenish because it was fluxed with potash containing potassium carbonate obtained by burning plants; the first true northern European style was called *Verre de fougère* (fern glass) in France and Belgium, and *Waldglas* (forest glass) in German-speaking areas. By contrast, Mediterranean glass-makers used sodium carbonate, which they took from seaweed.

One example of the originality of the Teutonic style is a long conical glass with a small base and such strange ornamentation that it looks like an elephant's trunk; others are a drinking-horn, sometimes smooth and usually decorated with thin lines, and an embossed glass called a *Römer,* perhaps because it was influenced by a style popular towards the end of the Roman Empire. Other products typical of the period include a type of small hanging lamp pierced at the very bottom by a ring or metal clasp, rounded goblets, portable flasks, and conical vases with inverted conical bases.

In the 13th and 14th centuries, Italian glass began to influence production in France, Germany, England, and Christian Spain. Glass-making was better organised and the quality of the materials greatly improved. There was utilitarian glassware – elegant bulb-shaped goblets and bottles with long necks, frequently seen in contemporary paintings and miniatures – and stained glass. Stained glass was made by a process similar to that used in Roman glazing: small pieces of glass were placed side by side in an iron frame, and were then moulded and painted at a high temperature. Up to the 14th century, stained glass was comparatively rare, although there are 8th- and 9th-century examples in the basilicas of St John Lateran and Sta Maria in Trastevere in Rome.

GREAT
BRITAIN

London●
Antwerp
Saxony

Normandy
Liège●
Cologne●
Hainault

Rouen●
St Germain
-en-Laye
Paris●
Seine
Meuse
Rhine
Thuringia
Silesia

●Nantes
GERMANY

Nevers●
Bavaria

FRANCE
Innsbruck● ●Hall

Rhône
Padua Murano
Lombardy
Genoa
Venice

SPAIN
Pyrenees
Provence
Ravenna

Catalonia
Bologna●
Florence

●Toledo
Barcelona
ITALY

Cordova
●Rome

Granada
Alicante
Naples●

Almería
SICILY

58

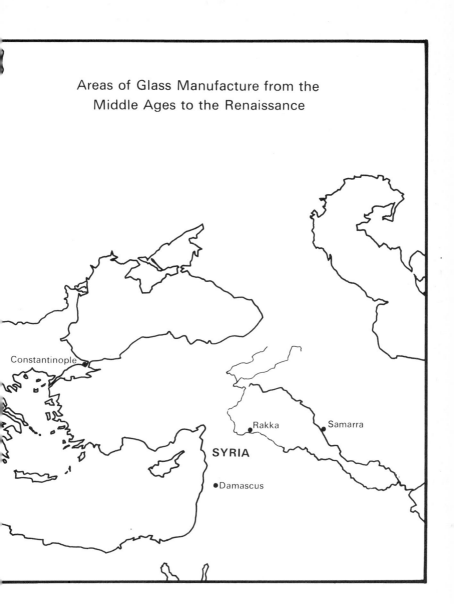

Areas of Glass Manufacture from the
Middle Ages to the Renaissance

Constantinople

Rakka   Samarra

SYRIA

●Damascus

VENICE AND THE RENAISSANCE

The art of glass-making may have been brought to Venice by the first inhabitants, who were driven from their homes on the Adriatic by pirates in the 7th and 8th centuries; or it may have been discovered during experiments carried out by monks, who were great alchemists; or it may have been a by-product of the making of mosaics. Whichever is the correct explanation, glass was certainly being made in Venice by the *fiolari* (glass-makers) before the year 1000. These glass-makers eventually formed themselves into a guild and (like painters, sculptors, architects, etc.) worked according to regulations laid down by the state; the first Glass-makers' Statute was passed in 1271. At the end of the century all glass-furnaces were removed to the nearby island of Murano because they had caused so many fires. Murano quickly began to flourish, thanks to increasing trade in the Mediterranean. In addition to receiving a certain autonomy from the state, Murano had its own government representatives and a *Libro d'oro,* (a Golden Book: a book written in gold letters, listing noble Venetian families and some foreign princes. Only the families in this book could be elected to high government and legal positions; many important glass-makers were included in this *Libro d'oro*, which meant they could marry into the aristocracy.

Very little is known about Murano in the 13th and 14th centuries, except for a few names and descriptions of how the work was organised, but the glassware cannot have been very different from that produced elsewhere in the West. However, miniatures, frescoes and mosaics of the period have been discovered, and glass pastes manufactured on Murano were used to make *tesserae* for mosaics. These *tesserae* came in a wide variety of colours, but particularly in gold since this was the colour used for backgrounds. In the 13th century, walls and domes were decorated with mosaics in Ravenna and towns on the Adriatic, although the best mosaics had been done in the 11th and 12th centuries and can be seen in the Venetian churches of S. Teodoro, S. Giacomo di Rialto, S. Nicolo di Lido, S. Cipriano di Murano, and of course in St Mark's Cathedral. The demand for *tessarae* in Venice was enormous between the 9th and 13th centuries, and

Two engravings depicting a 15th century glass furnace, from
De Re Metallica, by Georg Bauer (1494-1555), published in
Basel in 1556. Science Museum, London. On the left:
A - Blow-pipe. B - Little Window. C - Marble. D - Forceps.
E - Moulds by means of which the shapes are produced.
Upon: A - Arches of the second furnace. B - Mouth of the
lower chamber. C - Windows of the upper chamber.
D - Big-bellied pots. E - Mouth of the third furnace.
F - Recesses for the receptacles. G - Openings in the upper
chamber. H - Oblong receptacles.

Murano may well have supplied other towns, including Ravenna.

An important technical advance was the development – possibly the invention – of lenses by the rock crystal engravers, who were in a different guild from the glass-makers. This was, however, overshadowed by the development of glass-blowing. It is uncertain how this was handed down from Roman times, but it was to be the beginning of the Murano tradition.

It may seem strange that so little is known about Murano in the 14th century, but it must be remembered that nobody thought of preserving cheap, breakable objects. When more valuable glassware began to be produced it was very carefully looked after. From the 15th century onwards glass either is dated or can be dated fairly accurately. This glassware had an elegance not normally expected of work by simple craftsmen, and it formed part of a great cultural movement to which Venice made an important contribution. It is fair to say that glass was more important than any of the other minor arts.

One of the glories of Murano, and indeed of all Venetian art, was a wonderful sense of colour. The

17. Vase. Roman-Syrian (?). 1st century AD. Museo Vetrario, Murano.

18. Plate. Roman-Alexandrian. 1st century AD. Museo
Vetrario, Murano.

19. Drinking cup. Alexandrian. 4th century AD. Museo Civico Archeologico, Milan.

20. Situla. Alexandrian. 3rd-4th century AD. Treasury, St. Mark's Cathedral, Venice.

21. Vase. Roman-Alexandrian. 1st century AD. Corning
Museum of Glass, New York. Donated by Arthur Houghton.

22. Ointment vase. Alexandrian. 4th century AD. Victoria and Albert Museum, London. Photo: John Webb.

23. Cross (detail). Hellenistic. 3rd-4th century AD. Civico
Museo Cristiano, Brescia.

24. Vase. Syrian. 9th century. Kunstgewerbemuseum, Cologne.

25. Drinking cup. Byzantine. 10th century. Treasury,
St Mark's Cathedral, Venice.

26. Vase. Syrian. *c.* 10th century. Kunstgewerbemuseum, Cologne.

27. Drinking bowl. Islamic. Early 9th century. Treasury,
St Mark's Cathedral, Venice.

28. Glass. Alexandrian. 12th century. Kunstsammlungen, Veste Coburg, West Germany.

29. Bottle. Byzantine or Alexandrian. *c.* 8th century. Victoria and Albert Museum, London. Photo: John Webb.

30. Glass. Islamic. c. 10th century. Nationalmuseet, Copenhagen.

31. Bottle. Islamic, probably from Iraq. 9th-10th century. Victoria and Albert Museum, London. Photo: John Webb.

32. Ointment jar. Syrian-Mesopotamian 'Aleppo' glassware.
13th century. Museo Civico, Bologna. Photo: Fotofast.

33. Glass. Syrian 'Aleppo' glassware. 13th century.
Kunstgewerbemuseum, Cologne.

34. Flask. Syrian 'Damascus' glassware. 13th-14th century.
Freer Gallery of Art, Washington.

35. Mosque lamp. Syrian. 14th century. Kunstgewerbemuseum, Cologne.

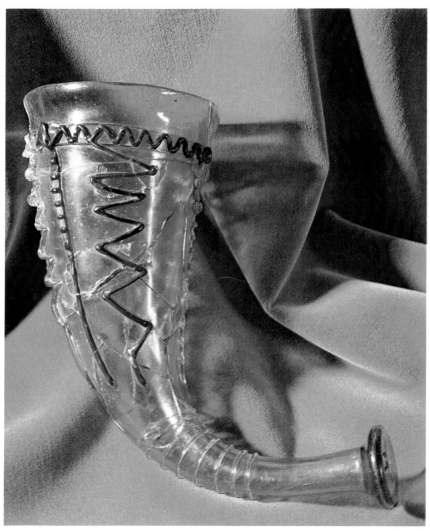

36. Drinking horn. Central European. 4th-5th century.
Römisch-Germanisches Museum, Cologne.

37. Chalice. Late Roman (Rhenish). 4th century.
Römisch-Germanisches Museum, Cologne.

38. Drinking vessel. Rhenish. 7th-9th century. Musée des Beaux-Arts, Rouen.

39. The Barovier Goblet. Murano. Late 15th century. Museo Vetrario, Murano.

40. Goblet. Murano. Late 15th century. Museo Civico,
Bologna. Photo: Fotofast.

41. Goblet. Murano. Late 15th century. Kunstgewerbemuseum,
Cologne.

42. Plate. Murano. Late 15th century. Museo Nazionale, Trento.

43. Reliquary. Murano. Late 15th century. Museo Vetrario, Murano.

44. Marriage cup. Murano. Late 15th century. Museo
Vetrario, Murano.

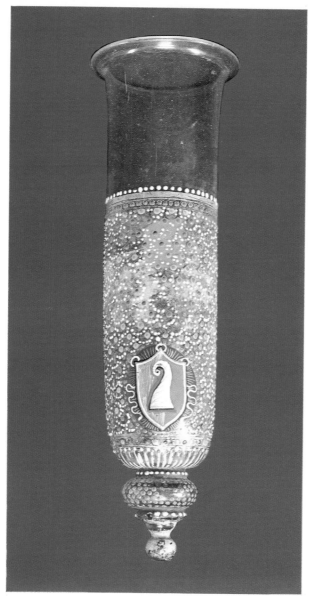

45. Hanging lamp. Murano. Late 15th-early 16th century.
Museo Vetrario, Murano.

46. Plate. Murano. Late 16th century. Museo Vetrario, Murano.

47. Flask. Murano. Late 15th century. Museo Civico, Bologna.
Photo: Fotofast.

48. Chalice. Murano. Early 16th century. Museo Vetrario, Murano.

traditional ability of Venetian craftsmen to imitate precious stones meant that it was natural for them to produce glass in a wide range of colours. For this reason, expensive glass of the early Renaissance was coloured rather than transparent – usually dark blue, amethyst red, emerald green or opaque white. It was most frequently made as an engagement or wedding present, or in praise of a great man, though it was occasionally religious. The decoration might take the form of a portrait surrounded in the Renaissance manner with medallions or floral crowns. Sometimes there were more complex mythological or allegorical scenes (for example, Faith, Justice and Hope), sometimes pictures of loved ones or knights and ladies. These designs were glazed at a high temperature after the bowl of the object had cooled. The technique was the same as that used on Islamic glass, which is not surprising in view of the strong commercial and cultural links between Venice and the Levant. (Arab influence on architecture had been evident since the end of the 3rd century, and themes and designs related to Islamic art were used even by 15th-century painters.)

The designs on early Murano glass were frequently inspired by contemporary architecture, sculpture and literature. A particularly influential book was Francesco Colonna's *Hypnerotomachia Poliphili*, published in 1499; it was written in praise of beauty and was composed in the humanist style with an abundance of symbols and literary references. The finest examples of Murano glass of this period are a marriage cup in the British Museum, the Barovier Goblet in the Murano Museum, and an opaque white goblet at Trento, northern Italy.

It is impossible to decide which craftsmen were responsible for early Murano glassware, although the Barovier Goblet is called after a craftsman of that name who is known for his glazing. Contemporary painters, architects and sculptors certainly influenced the designing of glassware. This is not surprising in view of the fact that some of the greatest 15th-century Venetian painters came from Murano, for example the Vivarini and Mocetto families, Andrea da Murano and Quirizio da Murano. Bartolomeo Vivarini and Girolamo Mocetto worked in stained glass and are believed to have designed the famous window in the church of

SS Giovanni e Paolo in Venice. Although this is the only major example in this part of Italy, stained glass undoubtedly maintained its popularity.

Glass-making also benefited from scientific experiments carried out in Venice and Padua. The ground was prepared by Anzolo Barovier (d. 1460), the first important member of what was to be a famous family of glass-makers. Barovier moved in humanist circles and knew the most celebrated scientists of his time. As a result of his contacts with the Athenaeum in Padua and philosophers and humanists of the Rialto School, many important technical developments occurred in glass-making and a great deal of research into new processes was undertaken. It was probably due to the efforts of Barovier that *cristallo*, a very clear colourless glass, was developed on Murano.

Crystal glass was first used to make objects like those that had been decorated by glazing – elegant marriage cups, large plates, chalices and vases. Indeed the designs on crystal glass were not new at all and the decorating process was also the same, although it was done with greater accuracy. Later designs include fish-scales (probably copied from mosaics), wavy lines, minute rectangular shapes, religious or allegorical scenes, portraits, and the escutcheon of the dedicatee. Splendid examples from this period are the two flasks with the Bentivoglio crest in the Museo Civico, Bologna, and the Sforzesco Chalice in Milan Castle. Another typical 15th-century piece was a large bowl probably used for fruit: it was long and round at the top, and had wide conical legs.

Pottery and metalwork inspired much crystal glass work at this time – for example plates with a ribbed design, goblets with a bean-shaped motif on legs sprayed with gold leaf, and *cesendelli* (cylindrical oil lamps) – and traditional colour schemes remained popular into the 16th century. Although colourless glass could now be made, other materials were still being manufactured, either to imitate semi-precious stones like chalcedony (a kind of quartz), malachite and agate, or to be sold to the makers of mosaics and beads; small 'pearls' were regularly exported to Africa and the Middle and Far East. *Lattimo* (milky white glass) was used to imitate maiolica earthenware and also porcelain, which Europeans learned how to manufacture only much later. It was decorated with a multicoloured design in some ways similar to the ornamentation on pilgrims' flasks and contemporary mosaics.

Very little is known about utilitarian glass made between the middle of the 15th century and the beginning of the 16th; but paintings of banquets by Bellini, Mantegna, Marziale, Crivelli and others show carefully designed and well proportioned cups and bowls. The most common design was a *buca*, a decanter for water or wine. The only two that have been found show very little advance in style on Medieval examples.

In the 16th century, the glass-making industry became even better organised. The previous law regulating the craft, which had been passed in the middle of the 15th century, was replaced by a *Mariegola*, a book of statutes awarded as an official recognition that the activity in question was an established part of the artistic and civic life of Venice. The glass-makers' *Mariegola* had a magnificent illuminated frontispiece. It laid down rules, as to how glass should be made and business transactions conducted, regulated the relationship between master and pupil, and set out terms of apprenticeship; it also made St Anthony the patron saint of glass-making. The *Mariegola* reveals many aspects of the social structure of Venice; it also demonstrates that the state continued to exercise great power through a bench of judges known as the Old Justice, sitting in Rialto, the main business centre.

Closer contacts between Venice and other parts of Italy led to the introduction of new Renaissance elements. In glassware, pictorial decoration – in particular the glazing of dark coloured glass – was superseded by the elegant moulding of transparent glass; in fact glass-making was probably more sensitive to cultural movements than any of the other 'industrial' arts.

From the beginning of the 16th century, more and more expensive glass was made at Murano; fortunately much of it has survived. The designs were frequently inspired by the paintings of Tintoretto and Veronese. And, conversely, the works of these painters, of the Bassano family, Bonifacio and others, document countless chalices, goblets, cups, plates, bottles and glasses. Murano glassware was extremely elegant and well proportioned: chalices were long and slender, goblets had baluster stems copied from architectural designs, flasks were narrow in the middle as in the pre-Renaissance style, bottles were in the traditional bulb shape or else had square bases. There were also amphoras, decanters with spouts and curved handles, fruit-dishes with lids, large ornamental vases, perfume containers and small cups. Colour (usually bright blue) was sometimes used to decorate the legs of chalices, the handles of small cups, brims and bases. Another example of the imaginativeness of the early 16th century is a boat-shaped water decanter, probably first made by Armenia Vivarini, the daughter of the painter Alvise Vivarini. Towards the end of the century, lamps, phials and vases were shaped after the Roman manner, like ponies, rats or imaginary creatures, and decorated with raised borders, crests, and spiral or zig-zag motifs in the same material as the objects they decorated; they clearly herald the advent of the Baroque.

The Renaissance was a period of intense interest in techniques, and many books about glass were written, including the treatises of Filarete and Leon Battista Alberti, and Biringuccio's *Pirotechnia,* published in

Venice in 1540. Materials continued to be improved, for example the impastation for beads and mosaics (although mosaics were now losing their popularity) and the glass pastes for imitation precious stones. Transparent glass was sometimes covered with interwoven, spirally twisted or horizontal threads of blown *lattimo* (milky white glass) which was occasionally engraved with *decorazioni a piume* or *decorazioni a penna* (pen decorations). This new technique was called *reticello* or *filigrana* (filigree: ornamental lacework design), and was used to make plates for use at table or for display, vases, fruit bowls and other dishes used in aristocratic homes. The last important new 16th-century technique was crackle-glass (more properly called ice-glass), which was made by plunging the glass into cold water while it was still very hot; the result was an opaque glass covered with a fine network of lines. This could be decorated in the normal way, or by contrasting the crackled parts with areas that were smooth and transparent.

Craftsmen at Murano also revived and improved the old technique of decorating glass some time after it had been moulded. Plates, fruit bowls, goblets and display pieces were made of glass that was transparent, dark red or dark blue; then palm trees, small branches, damask roses or intricate geometrical designs were traced along the border with the point of a diamond or flint. Very occasionally figurative designs were used on religious or commemorative glassware. This method had the delicacy of lace-work, though it was inferior to contemporary Flemish and Dutch work. Sometimes pictures were added to glass that had already been moulded; this process superseded glazing and was a quick and easy method of producing transparent pictures of all sizes on picture-frames, travelling chests and liturgical vestments. These pictures resembled *églomisé* glass, which was covered with gold leaf incised by a pointed instrument; the design was protected by a piece of thin glass which was fused over it. The fact that diamond-point decoration could be carried out anywhere – not necessarily at a glass-furnace – no doubt contributed to its popularity with goldsmiths in other parts of Italy. In the 15th and 16th centuries in the Veneto, Emilia, Lombardy and Tuscany, this process was also used to decorate osculatories (pictures of Christ or the Virgin Mary, formerly kissed by the priest and the people during Mass) and religious or secular diptychs. The decorations were mythological, allegorical or religious, and were frequently copied directly from contemporary paintings and engravings. Engravings by Marcantonio Raimondi, by other artists working with Giorgione and Titian, and by Dürer exerted a strong influence on 16th-century glass decoration.

At the beginning of the 16th century, the Dal Gallo brothers of Murano took out a patent on crystal looking-glasses. Mirrors already existed – had possibly existed since ancient times – but until this time they had always been made of steel or polished silver. The new process involved laying tinfoil on a piece of glass and then rubbing in mercury until the two metals amalgamated. In spite of their usefulness, very few looking-glasses were made until the following century.

Although Murano was the leading glass centre throughout the Renaissance, it was by no means the only one in Italy. Florence and Altare were the most important after Murano, but there were many other centres in the north of Italy (in Padua, Verona, Vicenza, Ferrara and Lombardy) and further to the south (in Naples, Arezzo, Pistoia, and Figline in the valley of the Arno), although their products were on the whole not very imaginative.

Glass-making prospered in Florence thanks to the Medici, the ruling family, and at times its products even rivalled those of Murano. Protective laws kept the importation of Venetian crystal glass to a minimum, and attempts were made to imitate it. Although Murano craftsmen were strictly forbidden to emigrate, some were lured away to other Italian towns, and even abroad, to teach the secrets of their craft. In the early 16th century, these fugitive glass-makers usually confined themselves to making ordinary glassware. In the late 16th and early 17th centuries, Florence began to manufacture glass for medical and scientific purposes; the Science Museum there has a fine collection of containers like medicine bottles and test-tubes, and there are even alcohol thermometers, barometers and lenses. In this period, artistic and technical standards rose considerably and, except for a certain sameness in design and the impurity of the materials, glass from Florence was quite as good as that from Venice.

The other major centre of glass-making was Altare,

a small town near Genoa. Unfortunately, no authenticated Altare glass has been found. Historical documents show that there was a very old guild of craftsmen that was reorganised in the 15th century and called 'The University of the Art of Glass-making'; as at Murano, glass-makers had a high status. But unlike the craftsmen of Murano, they were allowed to emigrate, and the town even prided itself on giving the number of its master craftsmen in other parts of Europe. They even worked on Murano, and made important contributions to the making of mirrors and to glass-blowing techniques.

THE *FAÇON DE VENISE* IN EUROPE

The *façon de Venise*, or Venetian style of glass-making, developed from the middle of the 16th century and flourished throughout the 17th century, influencing all European countries. Towards the end of the 16th century, when Renaissance styles gave way to the Baroque, glass became very ornate. The great increase in political, economic and cultural relations between countries meant that Murano's influence was much more widely felt, with all countries colouring their glass – and, as a result, that schools which would eventually rival Murano were brought into being.

The Venetians themselves copied some foreign designs, including the German *Kuttrolf*, which they made into a long-necked vase, and *Maigelein*, also German, which they made into a beaker with an undulating shape. Since early Medieval times, northern European countries had decorated their glass by using the same material as the object or by using different colours; they soldered the decoration on to give the effect of sculpture or chiaroscuro. Murano glass now began to be decorated in the same way, and the process became international and characteristic of the whole 17th century.

One piece of late Renaissance glass that anticipated the Baroque was the *calice ad alette* or *calice a serpenti* (winged glass or serpent glass); the stem was colourfully adorned with leaves, twigs and small flowers, or circles and other symmetrical designs. Exactly when this glass first influenced designs outside Italy is unknown, but it was to be the hallmark of Venetian glass throughout Europe. It is even more difficult to date all *reticello* and any *graffito* done just before or just after the beginning of the 17th century, because there are no dates, signatures or other marks. These designs were extremely common among the Flemish glass-makers, the Germans (who called it *Flügelglas*), and many others; all the best surviving examples would appear to date from the end of the 16th century, though the shapes and elaborate decoration suggest the Baroque period.

The *façon de Venise* existed mainly because Murano glass was exported on a large scale in the 16th century. On the other hand, the Venetians feared competition, and glass-makers in the rest of Europe were anxious to rival the artistic and technical supremacy of Murano. Much of the competition came from fellow-Italians (from Altare in particular) who emigrated to France, Belgium or England. As we have seen, there were even some Murano craftsmen who risked severe punishment by leaving Venice. By the end of the 16th century, many countries had Italians making glass for them. France was one of the first, with craftsmen from Altare and Venice working in Paris, St Germain-en-Laye, Rouen, Nantes and Nevers. In the Low Countries, there were Venetians at Antwerp, Liège and Brussels. At Hainault, the Colinet family were making excellent imitations of Murano glass in the middle of the 16th century; the catalogue (1550–1555) of one of their glassworks lists a number of types of glass later adopted at Murano, including the very tall, narrow wine glass called a *flute*. Of those who came over to England during the reign of Elizabeth I, the most distinguished was Jacopo Verzelini. He used materials similar to Murano *cristallo*, decorating it with the point of a diamond. Much of his work is preserved, and the earliest date on any piece is 1577. There were also glass-makers in Sweden from the middle of the 16th century.

The most famous Austrian centre, at Hall in the Tyrol, produced glass similar in form and design to that of Murano. Cups, goblets, reliquaries and pyxes were decorated in *graffito* and were painted with gold and other colours. The part of Spain most influenced by Venice was Catalonia, and Barcelona in particular;

there, transparent glass was skilfully used to make travelling flasks, goblets and sweet-meat boxes. Even more typically Venetian objects were the *almorrata* (a rose-water sprinkler with several spouts) and the *porron* (a bottle used in taverns). Later on, decoration was strongly influenced by Arab styles, the flowing lines and pictures of animals and birds characteristic of the *façon de Venise* being replaced by symmetrical designs glazed in a variety of colours. Outside Barcelona, the glass industry developed quickly; the towns of Alicante, Granada and Cadalso were given the title *de los vidrios* ('of glass'), and other important centres were Toledo and Almeria. In Castile, even in the 16th century, Baroque work was very popular. Brown or dark emerald glass was covered with fishes' fins, crests, rings and other strange designs, usually done by a moulding process.

The second half of the 16th century witnessed a great advance in the style and techniques of European glass. Craftsmen began to be aware of designs from countries other than their own, and particularly from Venice. Countries that had remained unaffected by foreign influences since the 10th century, even since

49. Lamp. Murano. Mid 16th century. Museo Vetrario, Murano.

50. Decanter. Murano. Early 16th century. Museo Vetrario, Murano.

51. Fruit bowl. Murano. Late 16th century. Museo Civico, Turin.

52. Bowl. Murano. Mid 16tn century. Museo Vetrario, Murano.

53. Fruit container. Murano. Late 16th century. Museo Vetrario, Murano.

54. Reliquary. Murano. Late 16th century. Museo Vetrario, Murano.

55. Fruit bowl. Murano. Mid 16th century. Museo Vetrario, Murano.

56. Pitcher. Murano. Mid 16th century. Museo Nazionale del
Bargello, Florence.

57. Glass. Murano. Late 16th century. Museo Vetrario, Murano.

58. Flask. Spanish (Barcelona). Late 15th-early 16th century.
Museo Vetrario, Murano.

59. Glass. Spanish (Barcelona). Late 15th-early 16th century. Museo Vetrario, Murano.

60. Bowl. Spanish. Early 16th century. Museos de Arte, Barcelona.

61. Glass. German. Late 15th century. Kunstgewerbemuseum,
Cologne.

62. Glass. German. Early 16th century. Kunstgewerbemuseum, Cologne.

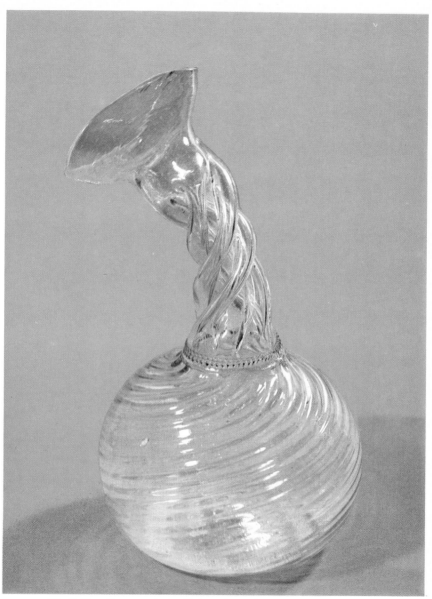

63. Bottle. German. Late 16th-early 17th century. Kunstgewerbemuseum, Cologne.

64. Glass. Rhenish. Late 16th-early 17th century.
Kunstgewerbemuseum, Cologne.

the late Roman Empire, now began to develop their own styles. One example, a colourless conical glass with no base and a slightly flared brim, can often be seen in Flemish paintings. Also common in the 16th century was a conical goblet with an inverted conical base; it was later adopted by Murano craftsmen. Popular in the north of Europe was a long cylindrical glass that was wide at the top and had conical legs; it was called a *Passglas* because it was passed from guest to guest at table.

Even the German *Römer* was popular well into the 19th century. It was also a glass for use at table, and could be either squat or tall and slender; it was attractively embossed, either all over or only at the bottom. This method of decoration was a characteristic of German work even during the period of great Italian influence. Another German design adopted in many European countries was the *Kuttrolf*, a bottle with one narrow neck or several thin ones, and a spout. It was popular from ancient times to the Baroque period, although the most elegant designs were made in the 16th century. In the 17th century, much German and French glassware was decorated by glazing in the Venetian manner: French *verres de mariage* (marriage cups) were completely covered with inscriptions and scrolls, although they were later influenced by Rhenish styles.

The *façon de Venise* inspired the stylistic and technical advances of the Renaissance and it is difficult to tell where much of the glassware of the period comes from, since craftsmen moved freely from country to country and imitated one another's work. By the end of the 16th century, glass was truly European in style.

LIST OF ILLUSTRATIONS

1   Amphoras and ointment jars. Greek, Egyptian, Roman, Palestinian. 5th century BC - 4th century AD. Museo di Capodimonte, Naples. These objects are technically similar, and it is difficult to date them precisely because they were used in all the Mediterranean cultures. They were popular even in Italy, and influenced Etruscan art. Hellenistic amphoras and ointment jars of the *alabastron* type were usually dark blue and decorated with straight or wavy lines.

2   Decorative sheet of glass. Roman-Alexandrian. 1st century AD. Victoria and Albert Museum, London. Photo: John Webb. This is made from the material used on mosaics, and decorated with figurative and floral designs. The Egyptians were very skilled at making these glass sheets, which they used as ornaments.

3   Necklace. Roman-Alexandrian. 1st century AD. Museo Vetrario, Murano. The Egyptians were the first people to make necklaces; the one illustrated here is made of small multi-coloured discs of glass paste decorated with white spiral lines. Some necklaces were even made in the 4th and 3rd centuries BC; this one was found in a tomb of the 1st century AD.

4   Pair of vases. Pre-Roman. 4th-3rd century BC. Museo Civico, Adria. Before the invention of glass-blowing, hollow objects were made by putting glass paste around moulds that were later broken. The two vessels in the illustration, perhaps the only ones of their type to survive, are made of pieces of glass placed horizontally and vertically. The inside is dark blue.

5   Vase. Alexandrian or Syrian, *c*. 1st century AD. Museo Vetrario, Murano. 'Murrhine vases', as vases of this type are called, were made by fusing differently coloured glass pastes; as in the illustration, they were decorated with long irregular lines on a white or light blue background.

6   Plaque. Roman-Alexandrian (?). 1st-2nd century AD. Victoria and Albert Museum, London. Photo: John Webb. This type of plaque could be decorated by moulding or pre-moulding, and the theme was often pagan: Bacchantes (as in the illustration), heads of Medusa, or gargoyles.

7   Bowl with two handles. Made by the Syrian craftsman Aristeas. Late 1st century AD. Castello Strada, Scaldasole, Pavia. The relief decoration is similar to that on a Roman *patera* (a shallow dish with handles). Very little glassware at any time has been signed by the craftsman; here the name is written in Greek and has been moulded on to the bowl.

8   Bowl with two handles. Alexandrian. 1st century AD. Museo Civico, Adria. In Roman times expensive glassware was often influenced by metal designs. This bowl is copied from a contemporary silver drinking vase, and the moulding is so skilled that it looks as though only a single piece of glass has been used.

9   Bowl. Alexandrian. 1st century AD. Museo Vetrario, Murano. This ribbed bowl without legs is made of extremely thin glass, and the decorations, moulded on while it was being blown, are *lattimo* (milky white) lines and dots. This kind of bowl was usually blue, amber or amethyst red.

10. Pitcher. Roman. 1st century AD. Museo Civico, Adria. Glassware of this period was frequently inspired by contemporary mosaic designs; the pitcher in the illustration is similar to a Greek terracotta *askos* (a kind of wine jar).

11. Vase. Roman. 2nd-3rd century AD. Victoria and Albert Museum, London. Photo: John Webb. Here again, metal plate has been the inspiration; the handle and one or two other details were probably moulded on.

12. Oil jar. Roman-Syrian. 1st-2nd century AD. Museo Vetario, Murano. The imitation of animals was very unusual at this time. The jar in the illustration is incomplete.

13. Glass. Roman. 1st-2nd century AD. Museo Vetrario, Murano. Roman glasses for use at table were often long and conical, and the flat surface was decorated with moulded bosses.

14. Glass. Syrian. 1st century AD. Museo Vetrario, Murano. A new technique enabled Syrian craftsmen to repeat a design (in this case letters and crowns of laurel) on the same object. The Greek inscription says 'The victory is yours'.

15. Drinking horn. Roman. 1st century AD. Museo Civico, Adria. A Greek drinking cup called a *rhytos* inspired this kind of horn, which took many forms and could be decorated in a variety of ways; this one has the stylised head of an animal, possibly a fawn.

16. Amphora. Phoenician. 6th century BC. Museo Civico, Bologna. Photo: Fotofast. This is a splendid example of glazing, executed before blowing had been invented. The form, the smooth surface (polished by a grindstone), the handles and the ribs are strongly reminiscent of metal amphoras.

17. Vase. Roman-Syrian (?). 1st century AD. Museo Vetrario, Murano. The stylised relief glazing suggests that this vase comes from the Middle East; it was found in a Dalmatian cemetery, but it might have been imported. The design is similar to that on Egyptian clay vases, which were decorated à *la barbotine* (with a special paste for adding ornamentation).

18. Plate. Roman-Alexandrian. 1st century AD. Museo Vetrario, Murano. This plate was moulded and then given an *intaglio* engraving; the oval design and the long flat perforated handles are in imitation of metalwork.

19. Drinking cup. Alexandrian. 4th century A D. Museo Civico Archeologico, Milan. This is one of the few examples of *diatreta* glassware to have been discovered. The inscription *'Bibe vivas multis annis'* ('Drink your fill and live long') suggests that it was intended for use rather than display. The series of connecting rings at the bottom was to protect the cup.

20. *Situla*. Alexandrian. 3rd-4th century A D. Treasury, St Mark's Cathedral, Venice. This is another example of *diatreta* glass; the hunting scene of horses, wild animals and huntsmen was worked in *intaglio*. A *situla* was a slightly tapering vase with a wide brim; it might or might not have handles.

21. Vase. Roman-Alexandrian. 1st century A D. Corning Museum of Glass, New York. Donated by Arthur Houghton. The engraving has been carried out on two layers of glass, creating a cameo effect. The decoration shows scenes from the life of Priapus.

22.   Ointment vase. Alexandrian. 4th century A D. Victoria and Albert Museum, London. Photo: John Webb. The design of this derives from the Greek *ariballos* (a container for bath oils); it was moulded and then polished on a grindstone.

23.   Cross (detail). Hellenistic. 3rd-4th century A D. Civico Museo Cristiano, Brescia. The three people in the picture are popularly thought to be Galla Placidia (daughter of the Emperor Theodosius) and her children, but they are in fact unknown. The picture bears the name of the artist in Greek: BOYNNEPI KEPAMI.

24. Vase. Syrian. 9th century. Kunstgewerbemuseum, Cologne. Moulding survived into the early Middle Ages in countries where glassware was undeveloped; this vase is typically Middle Eastern.

25.   Drinking cup. Byzantine. 10th century. Treasury, St Mark's Cathedral, Venice. The decoration of the whole cup is in the style of 4th-century Alexandrian glassware, and the themes of the pictures are mythological.

26.   Vase. Syrian, c. 10th century. Kunstgewerbemuseum, Cologne. Even in the Middle Ages, Syrian glassware was late Roman in style. This vase was decorated when the glass had cooled.

27.   Drinking bowl. Islamic. Early 9th century. Treasury, St Mark's Cathedral, Venice. The dark glass of these bowls has often been mistaken for another material, and the example illustrated looks as if it is made of turquoise. It could be Persian, for the stylised running hares resemble the decoration on some glassware found at Samarra. The gilded silver decoration at the top is in the Byzantine style of the 10th and 11th centuries.

28. Glass. Alexandrian. 12th century. Kunstsammlungen, Veste Coburg, West Germany. This is a Hedwig glass, one of a series named after St Hedwig, wife of the Prince of Silesia and protectress of Silesia and Poland. The decoration is in high relief and extremely stylised.

29. Bottle. Byzantine or Alexandrian, *c.* 8th century. Victoria and Albert Museum, London. Photo: John Webb. Two techniques were used to make this bottle: the shape and the flat surfaces were moulded, but the detail was carved with a grindstone. Circles in relief were typical of Byzantine glass at this time.

30. Glass. Islamic, *c.* 10th century. Nationalmuseet, Copenhagen. Islamic craftsmen learned glazing through contact with Byzantium. This glass was found in Denmark.

31. Bottle. Islamic, probably from Iraq. 9th-10th century. Victoria and Albert Museum, London. Photo: John Webb. The figurative decoration on this bottle was engraved in a way considered rather old-fashioned in Europe. The glass is transparent.

32. Ointment jar. Syrian-Mesopotamian 'Aleppo' glassware. 13th century. Museo Civico, Bologna. Photo: Fotofast. Jars of this type were made of dark blue glass and glazed in many colours, including gold. The inscription is in Arabic.

33. Glass. Syrian 'Aleppo' glassware. 13th century. Kunstgewerbemuseum, Cologne. The slightly flared brim is characteristic of 'Aleppo' glass; the wide band in the middle and stylised motifs were moulded on to the glass.

34. Flask. Syrian 'Damascus' glassware. 13th-14th century. Freer Gallery of Art, Washington. The Mongol occupation of Moslem countries influenced the decoration of much glassware of this period.

35. Mosque lamp. Syrian. 14th century. Kunstgewerbemuseum, Cologne. This is a typical hanging mosque lamp: vase-shaped, glazed and bearing Arabic crests and inscriptions. It comes from a Cairo mosque, although it was certainly imported.

36. Drinking horn. Central European. 4th-5th century. Römisch-Germanisches Museum, Cologne. The thread-like enamelled decoration was added while the dark green glass was still hot.

37. Chalice. Late Roman (Rhenish). 4th century. Römisch-Germanisches Museum, Cologne. This graceful chalice combines two modes of decoration: glazed parallel lines and openwork curved lines. It is known as the sea-shell chalice.

38. Drinking vessel. Rhenish. 7th-9th century. Musée des Beaux-Arts, Rouen. This is an example of Teutonic glass, which was manufactured in Germany and all the areas of northern Europe that came under German influence. Such glasses, usually dark green, were frequently decorated with inverted tear shapes.

39. The Barovier Goblet. Murano. Late 15th century. Museo Vetrario, Murano. This goblet was made to commemorate a marriage; the man and woman are shown in medallions on the side of the goblet. It is an outstanding example of expensive Venetian glassware of the early Renaissance. The moulded decoration, as delicate as that on a miniature, depicts allegories of Youth: the Fountain of Love and a cavalcade.

40. Goblet. Murano. Late 15th century. Museo Civico, Bologna. Photo: Fotofast. Metalwork clearly inspired the shape, the bean motif at the bottom of the bowl, the spherical knob halfway down, and the wide conical base. There are two scenes — the Adoration of the Magi and the Flight into Egypt — and two medallions each with the bust of a prophet.

41. Goblet. Murano. Late 15th century. Kunstgewerbemuseum, Cologne. This goblet is decorated in great detail, and with an accuracy more usual in a much later period than the 15th century.

42. Plate. Murano. Late 15th century. Museo Nazionale, Trento. Glass painting gradually became popular throughout Europe at the beginning of the 15th century; in the illustration, the graceful head of a girl is surrounded by birds, peacocks and vine-leaves.

43. Reliquary. Murano. Late 15th century. Museo Vetrario, Murano. This reliquary, with its rounded lid and cross, is copied from a metal one. The glazed dots and lines form a geometrical pattern.

44. Marriage cup. Murano. Late 15th century. Museo Vetrario, Murano. Marriage cups were usually bowl-shaped and had a broad base, which enabled them to be used as dishes for fruit or sweetmeats. The glass is transparent and is covered with a geometrical pattern of dots and short lines.

45. Hanging lamp. Murano. Late 15th-early 16th century. Museo Vetrario, Murano. This cylindrical hanging lamp is copied from a metal *cesendello* (oil lamp); the dots are arranged in a fish-scale design. The escutcheon is that of the Tiepolo family, who were Venetian nobles.

46. Plate. Murano. Late 16th century. Museo Vetrario, Murano. This is similar to the metal plates used at table in rich Venetian homes. It is ribbed and has a raised border, and is decorated in tasteful Renaissance style; the escutcheon is that of the Barbarigo family, who ruled Venice at the end of the 16th century.

47. Flask. Murano. Late 15th century. Museo Civico, Bologna. Photo: Fotofast. This is an imitation of the portable flasks taken on pilgrimages to the Holy Land, although these were usually made of terracotta or metal. The two flasks in the Museo Civico, Bologna, bear the Sforza and Bentivoglio crests, in honour of a marriage between the two families.

48. Chalice. Murano. Early 16th century. Museo Vetrario, Murano. A superb example of elegant crystal glass. This type of chalice is often found in the paintings of Veronese, Tintoretto and the Bassano family.

49. Lamp. Murano. Mid 16th century. Museo Vetrario, Murano. It required astonishing skill to make a lamp of this type. This one is in the shape of a pony; others were shaped like rats or mice. The type is reminiscent of Roman glassware.

50. Decanter. Murano. Early 16th century. Museo Vetrario, Murano. Water decanters shaped like ships were probably first made by Armenia Vivarini, the daughter of the painter Alvise Vivarini.

51. Fruit bowl. Murano. Late 16th century. Museo Civico, Turin. This bowl is one of the many types of reticulated work. The central picture, painted on the bottom of the dish, is elegantly surrounded by a ribbed design.

52. Bowl. Murano. Mid 16th century. Museo Vetrario, Murano. Like the two previous illustrations, a fine example of *reticello*, the milky white threads making a beautiful contrast with the dark transparent background.

53. Fruit container. Murano. Late 16th century. Museo Vetrario, Murano. The eagle motif (possibly heraldic) and the other designs on the lid are executed with the point of a diamond or flint.

54. Reliquary. Murano. Late 16th century. Museo Vetrario, Murano. Occasionally even liturgical objects were incised with a sharp stone. This reliquary, found at the Church of S. Martino on Burano, an island near Murano, is also decorated with a few small gilded pictures.

55.   Fruit bowl. Murano. Mid 16th century. Museo Vetrario, Murano. The surface is characteristic of crackle-glass, a process often used for ware of this type.

56.   Pitcher. Murano. Mid 16th century. Museo Nazionale del Bargello, Florence. Coloured glass pastes were often used to imitate precious stones and marble. This pitcher is imitation chalcedony.

57.   Glass. Murano. Late 16th century. Museo Vetrario, Murano. This is an early example of the *calice ad alette* (winged cup); the decorated perforations at the base were to become one of the hall marks of the *façon de Venise.*

58.   Flask. Spanish (Barcelona). Late 15th-early 16th century. Museo Vetrario, Murano. This is typical of polychrome glazing in the Spanish style. The decoration shows Eastern influence and is divided into four areas.

59.   Glass. Spanish (Barcelona). Late 15th-early 16th century. Museo Vetrario, Murano. This glass, like the flask in the previous illustration, is decorated with leaves and animals.

60. Bowl. Spanish. Early 16th century. Museos de Arte, Barcelona. The custom of using coloured and plain transparent glass together is Islamic in origin, but the technique employed here is a Venetian one. This bowl may have been intended for secular or religious purposes.

61. Glass. German. Late 15th century. Kunstgewerbemuseum, Cologne. This sort of glass is known as a *Maigelein*;
the ribbed design can be found on a good deal of 15th-century
glassware, drinking glasses in particular.

62. Glass. German. Early 16th century. Kunstgewerbemuseum, Cologne. This is a *Passglas*, a glass handed from one
guest to the next; the hoops indicated how much each guest
could drink. The overall green colour is characteristic of Central
European glass, but the darker bosses have no special historical
importance.

63. Bottle. German. Late 16th-early 17th century. Kunstgewerbemuseum, Cologne. This is a *Kuttrolf*, partly influenced
by Murano styles.

64. Glass. Rhenish. Late 16th-early 17th century. Kunstgewerbemuseum, Cologne. The *Römer*, as this type of glass is called,
had a conical base and bosses in the middle to make it easy to
grip; it was particularly common in the Rhine valley, a great
wine-producing area.